TITLE PAGE

Step by Step Affiliate Marketing Guide to Make Money Online from Home

For Students, House wives and Entrepreneurs.

Complete Step by Step Affiliate Marketing Guide from Getting Started to Making your First Sale to Getting Paid.

By Murtaza Lanewala

Author & CEO

For

WWW.ACCASUPPORT.COM

CLAIM YOUR BONUS EBOOK

To download your **Work from Home Methods Unleashed eBook**, click the below link.

Work From Home Methods Unleashed or copy/paste the below link

http://accasupport.com/work-from-home-methods-unleashed-free-download/

PREFACE

Step by Step Affiliate Marketing Guide to Make Money Online from Home is **NOT another boring ebook** on affiliate marketing which takes hundreds of hours to read and makes you overwhelmed with information overload and leaves you undecided on what to do and from where to start. Rather, it is a **complete step by step affiliate marketing guide from getting started to making your first sale to getting paid**. It provides step by step instructions; you just need to **follow the instructions exactly as given in the guide**. Remember, that you will **NOT be investing any significant amount money** during this process. It **assumes NO knowledge** of internet and affiliate marketing. It is a complete guide for beginners with **NO knowledge of affiliate marketing** to **making you a complete affiliate marketing professional**. It is a comprehensive and effective affiliate marketing guide with what you **can start making money within 48 hours.**

This guide is especially useful for those who:

- ❖ want **freedom,**
- ❖ are an entrepreneur and **want to become a CEO of his/her own business,**
- ❖ are looking for a **side business** to boost his/her monthly income,
- ❖ are **housewife** and cannot leave home but still want to become independent,
- ❖ are **student** and want to fund his/her education,
- ❖ are **retired person** and want to keep him or herself busy,
- ❖ are in **financial difficulty** and want to repair his/her debt but do not have any money. Please keep in mind that this guide is not about repairing debt.
- ❖ are highly motivated person and **want to achieve something worthwhile** in life,
- ❖ want to **get rid of his/her boring job.**
- ❖ want to **get rid of his/her stupid boss,**
- ❖ are jobless and **currently finding a job.**

Please do not leave your job until you are earning sufficient amount of money and have a future plan in place and do not investment any significant amount of money that you cannot afford to lose.

TABLE OF CONTENTS

TITLE PAGE 1

CLAIM YOUR BONUS EBOOK 3

PREFACE 4

TABLE OF CONTENTS 6

Part A: AFFILIATES 16

Step 1: BASICS OF AFFILIATE MARKETING 17

    1   What Is Affiliate Marketing? 17

    2   What Are The Benefits Of Affiliate Marketing? 18

    3   Is Affiliate Marketing For Me? 19

    4   Top Reasons Why You Need To Do Affiliate Marketing? 22

    5   Future Of Affiliate Marketing 23

6	Types Of Affiliate Marketing Programs	23
7	How Affiliate Marketing Works?	25
8	How To Do Affiliate Marketing?	26

Step 2: SELECTING AFFILIATE PROGRAM & PRODUCTS ... 28

1	Selecting Market Place Or Affiliate Program	28
2	How To Select Vendor/Affiliate Product?	29
3	Best Products For Affiliate Marketing	32

Step 3: AFFILIATE MARKETING STRATEGIES ... 34

1	What is Market and Market Niche?	34
2	Market or Market Niche	35
3	Selecting Market Niche	38
4	What is Market Segment?	41
5	Market or Market Segment	41
6	Selecting Market Segment	42

7 Affiliate Marketing Strategies 44

    7.1 Free eBooks 46

    7.2 Email Marketing 49

    7.3 Forums 55

    7.4 Social Media Marketing 57

    7.5 Video Marketing 59

    7.6 Blogs/Websites 61

    7.7 SEO (Search Engine Optimization) 64

    7.8 Article Marketing 65

    7.9 RSS Feeds 67

    7.10 Paid Advertising 68

8 Matching Internet Marketing Strategy with Affiliate Product 73

9 New Visitors or Existing Visitors 74

- 9.1 Cost 75
- 9.2 Market niche 75
- 9.3 Existing Strategies 76
- 9.4 Access to Affiliate Programs 76
- 9.5 Market size 77
- 9.6 Risk 77
- 10 Know Your Customer 78
- 11 Purchase Cycle/Buying Funnel 79
  - 11.1 Awareness 79
  - 11.2 Knowledge 80
  - 11.3 Interest 80
  - 11.4 Introduction 81
  - 11.5 Preference 82
  - 11.6 Purchase 82

11.7 Review 83

12 Implications of Purchase Cycle for Keyword Selection 83

Step 4: CREATING PROMOTIONAL MATERIALS 86

1 Choosing Keywords For Promotional Materials 86

    1.1 Customer You Want To Target 86

    1.2 Marketing Budget or Time 87

    1.3 Stage Of Market Life Cycle 88

    1.4 Return on Investment 89

    1.5 Affiliate Marketing Strategy Adopted 89

2 Keywords Selection for Search Engine Optimization 90

3 Persuasive Copywriting 94

4 Best Content for Affiliate Marketing 96

- 4.1 Reviews 97
- 4.2 Product Price Comparisons 99
- 4.3 Lists 100
- 4.4 Problem Solving 101

5 Obtaining Promotional Contents 102
- 5.1 PLR 102
- 5.2 Public Domain Materials 104

6 Securing Contents from Theft 106

Step 5: BOOSTING AFFILIATE MARKETING 110

1 Productivity Tools and Techniques 110
- 1.1 URL Shortners 110
- 1.2 Auto Responders 112
- 1.3 Auto Poster Plugins 113
- 1.4 Automatic Social Submitter 113

- 2 Outsource or Automate 114
- 3 Common Mistakes Made by Affiliate Marketers. 115
  - 3.1 Not Creating his/her Own Blog/Website .. 115
  - 3.2 Not Capturing Email Addresses 116
- 4 Not Choosing Suitable Software for Web Design 117
  - 4.1 Offline Blog Post Editors 119
  - 4.2 Security & Backups 121
  - 4.3 Not Making Use Of Free Plugins And Productivity Tools. 122
  - 4.4 Non Compliance With Rules 122
- 5 VPN and Proxy Servers 123
- 6 Meta Tags 124
  - 6.1 Nofollow/Dofollow 126
  - 6.2 Meta Noindex 127

- 6.3 Meta Description 128
- 6.4 Meta Keyword.. 129
- 7 Managing Performance as Affiliate 129

Part B: VENDORS... 133

AFFILIATE MARKETING FOR VENDORS 134

- 1 Affiliate Marketing for Vendors 134
- 2 In-house or Outsourcing Affiliate Program.......... 135
- 3 How To Select Affiliate Program For Vendors 137
    - 3.1 Commission Spread 137
    - 3.2 Competition B/W Vendor in Market Niche 137
    - 3.3 Ranking Of Vendors 137
    - 3.4 Methods Of Getting Payment.................... 138
    - 3.5 Transaction Cost Of Getting Payment 139

3.6   Payout Threshold 140

3.7   Payment Options For Buyers 141

3.8   Taxes 141

3.9   Initial Cost Of Signup 142

3.10   Number Of Webpages Or Websites Supported Per Account... 142

3.11   Integrating Accounts 143

3.12   Communication With Affiliates.................. 143

3.13   Statistical Information 143

3.14   Ease Of Purchase Processing 144

3.15   Terms Of Service 144

3.16   Countries Supported 144

3.17   Access to Customer Information 145

4   How To Attract High Quality Affiliates................. 145

    4.1   Provide Affiliates With Generous Commission 145

    4.2   Provide Affiliates With Multi-Tier Affiliate Program 146

    4.3   Provide Affiliate Tools & Resources 147

5   Maintaining Relationship with Affiliates 147

6   Setting Amount of Commission 148

    6.1   Number of Products 148

    6.2   Level of Competition 148

    6.3   Type of Products 148

    6.4   Resources 149

    6.5   Reputation from Existing Business 149

COPYRIGHT NOTICE 151

Part A: AFFILIATES

Step 1: BASICS OF AFFILIATE MARKETING

1 What Is Affiliate Marketing?

Affiliate Marketing is making your visitors or followers perform specific action, such as sale completed, form signup, click on link to vendor website etc. Reward varies depending on the task required. Tasks involving more risk of non-payment such as sales completed carry higher commission. Tasks such as click on vendor link carries lower commission per task performed.

Usually affiliate marketing involves commission % or flat fee per sale completed.

Affiliate marketing online is one of the internet marketing strategies available to vendors. On the other hand, affiliate marketing is monetization strategy for affiliate marketers. Affiliate marketers have to adopt other internet marketing strategies to make money via affiliate marketing.

2 What Are The Benefits Of Affiliate Marketing?

There are some of the benefits of affiliate marketing:

- ❖ Start with zero or little investment.
- ❖ Do it part time or full time. Do your existing job or business, complete your studies, take care of your parents and children, enjoy social life etc.

- ❖ Say good bye to your boring 9:00 am to 5:00 pm job.
- ❖ Do it from anywhere in the world such as from home or office or school (in free periods off course).
- ❖ No need for day to day management. You can make money while enjoying vacation or sleeping. You can resume your business from where you have left. Online affiliate marketing is an automated process in which visitor clicks on your affiliate link and on purchase affiliate marketer gets the commission and customer gets the product.

You do NOT need to develop the product, ship the product and provide after sales service etc.

- Unlimited earning potential and growth opportunities. Promote as many products as you want. There are hundreds of marketplaces and affiliate programs and thousands of products to promote.
- Get paid up to 90% commission on each sale at some affiliate marketplaces. It is the affiliate marketer who makes most out of each sale.

3   Is Affiliate Marketing For Me?

Affiliate marketing is for anyone who has:

- PC or Laptop or Smart Phone.
- Internet connection.
- Good at connecting with people.
- Bank account.

If you have an existing social media account such as Facebook or blog, you can make money referring products to your friends or visitors.

NO academic qualification or certification required.

You do NOT need to have good English.

NO experience required.

Fortunately, it does not require any eligibility criteria. It does not mean that affiliate marketing is easy money. It requires time and hard work to learn internet marketing skills. It cannot make you millionaire overnight. Therefore, please do not quit your job until you start earning sufficient amount of money.

You DO NOT need to have your own product. You can promote others product. In affiliate marketing you can choose among thousands of products. If one product does not work well you can quickly switch to other product without losing any significant amount of money. Creating your own product takes time and resources. Affiliate marketing provides you an instant product. However, you have the choice to develop your own product. So that you can keep 100% of the sale price and have an army of affiliate marketers promoting products for you.

Many affiliate marketing programs do not require you to maintain your own paid domain, blog or website. Affiliate marketer can make use of free blogging platforms such as wordpress.org (sophisticated), blogger.com (simple). Blogger.com lets you create your subdomain which will be the address of your blog. You can also use free web hosting providers to create blog or website using free software such as WordPress (wordpress.org). You can search the internet to find out free web hosting providers.

You DO NOT need any IT skills or specialized knowledge or background. If you can use Facebook or YouTube, you can create your own blog or website as well. Blog or website is not necessarily required to do affiliate marketing but it is recommended to have one from the beginning. I strongly recommend buying your own domain name regardless of which blogging platform (blogger.com or WordPress free software) do you use.

You DO NOT need to have in-depth knowledge of the product or market niche in which you are operating. However, you may need to do some research on your product and market niche to get started.

4   Top Reasons Why You Need To Do Affiliate Marketing?

- If you want freedom,
- If you are an entrepreneur and want to become a CEO of your own business,

- If you are looking for a side business to boost your monthly income,
- If you are housewife and cannot leave home but still want to become independent,
- If you are student and want to fund your education,
- If you are retired person and want to keep yourself busy,
- If you are in financial difficulty and want to repair your debt but do not have any money,
- If you are highly motivated person and want to achieve something worthwhile in your life,

- If people think you are worthless or loser,

- ❖ If you want to get rid of your boring job.
- ❖ If you want to get rid of your stupid boss,
- ❖ If you are jobless and currently finding a job,

then affiliate marketing is the right choice for you. You should definitely try affiliate marketing,

5 Future Of Affiliate Marketing

Affiliate marketing is 100% legitimate business and therefore your future is secured.

Now days more and more business are offering their products online. So, they need someone who can refer their products to potential customers. The more affiliate marketers they recruit the more they will earn. Therefore, they are offering massive commissions to affiliate marketers to attract and retain them.

6 Types Of Affiliate Marketing Programs

Affiliate marketing can have many tiers (levels). Affiliate marketing program in which affiliate receives commission for each sale made through his/her referral is 1st tier affiliate marketing program. It is the simplest form of affiliate marketing program.

More sophisticated affiliate marketing programs can have many tiers.

In 2 tier affiliate marketing, affiliate receives commission for each sale made through his/her referral as well as percentage of commission earned by 2nd tier affiliates. 2nd tier affiliates are those who joined affiliate program due to the referral of 1st tier affiliate. 2nd tier affiliates can have his/her own 2nd tier affiliates.

Example:

You joined an affiliate marketing program by my referral. Therefore, I will receive commission whenever you will get commission. My commission can be for example 2% of your commission.

Some affiliate marketing programs provides commission for sales made by affiliates up to 4 tiers.

7   How Affiliate Marketing Works?

Affiliate marketing involves the use of affiliate tracking software or scripts. Many open source and paid affiliate tracking softwares are available. Basically, all affiliate marketing softwares require the use of cookies.

Cookies are small scripts, which automatically gets installed on visitor's computer when visitor clicks on affiliate link generated by affiliate tracking software. It allows tracking the affiliate marketer who has place replaced his/her affiliate link to send the potential customer to vendor's website. If visitor has turned off cookies in his/her browser such as to protect his/her privacy, then affiliate will not get rewarded for sale.

Affiliate tracking software also apportions sale made by vendor due to referral from particular affiliate marketer using pre-set basis such as % of commission or flat fee.

8 How To Do Affiliate Marketing?

In this guide, I will guide you through the step by step process of making money via affiliate marketing. I will elaborate the following steps and provide you detailed guidance so that you can make informed decisions at each step of your affiliate marketing.

Step 1: Signup at affiliate marketplace. Some of the most popular market places are Shareasale.com, Amazon.com.

Step 2: Choose your market niche and product depending on your interests and skills.

Step 3: Open or use your existing social media account such as Facebook or setup a free blog at blogger.com.

Step 4: Generate your affiliate link. This link will contain your unique user id, so that you can be rewarded on each sale made through your referral.

Step 5: Spread a word about your affiliate product via social media or blog. Place your affiliate link in the posts.

Step 6: Take payment from affiliate marketplace. You can set payment frequency (daily, weekly, monthly) and mode of payment (bank transfer, check, PayPal) depending on payout method offered by affiliate marketplace.

Step 2:
SELECTING AFFILIATE PROGRAM & PRODUCTS

1   Selecting Market Place Or Affiliate Program

The following points should be kept in mind when selecting affiliate marketing program.

- ❖ Affiliate program should not require signup cost. They are already charging vendors for obtaining listing in the marketplace.
- ❖ Affiliate program should be able to make payment in your country.
- ❖ Affiliate program should have low payment threshold (such as $10 or $25) and high payment frequency (at least once a month). It will help you minimize the risk and meet your liabilities.
- ❖ Affiliate program should have good history of timely payments.

- ❖ Affiliate program should not be subject to excessive charges for releasing payment. It will decrease your net profit.

- ❖ Affiliate program should be available in the geo-location of your targeted customers.
- ❖ Affiliate program should have a good reputation. It can be determined by contacting other affiliates, searching on the web.
- ❖ Affiliate program provider should have sound future prospects.

2   How To Select Vendor/Affiliate Product?

- ❖ Vendor financial performance and position should be sound. If vendor go out of business than your marketing efforts go waste for that product. The way to deal with this problem is described later in this eBook.
- ❖ Affiliate product offered by the vendor should have good conversion rate. Conversion rate is the

number of visitors who landed at product page actually made a purchase. Attracting visitors takes time or money. Therefore, affiliate products with higher conversion rate provide more from your time and investment.

- Vendor should have good reputation. If vendor is involved in deceptive marketing and selling practice, then it will upset your existing contacts and they may leave you.
- Vendor product should be carefully priced. If vendor prices his/her product too high to attract affiliates, then it may not be able to convert referrals into sale. Therefore, you may lose commission as a result.
- % of commission offered by vendor. Higher commission means that you have higher share in value chain. Value chain is the suppliers involved in delivering product to the final customer. Increasing share of profit in value chain is fundamental to increase profitability.
- Vendor product should be viable and should not be subject to extra ordinary claims. It can be an

indication of deceptive marketing and selling practice.

- Some affiliate tracking software only allows tracking of vendor payment link on only 1 website. Therefore, if customer referred through your affiliate link buys by clicking on payment link on other website such as using redirection to redirect visitors to different website than you will lose commission. Vendor may do so to offer the same product at discounted price when visitor clicks the back button.
- Vendor should not have alternative payment links and offline payment options, which cannot identify sale to your referral. In that case, if customer purchase from alternative payment links, then you not get any reward. It includes entry and exist pop-ups.
- Affiliate program offered by vendor should be able to track your affiliate marketing efforts and able to make payments in timely manner.
- Vendor product should belong to market niche that you can promote taking account of your skills and

experience. However, it is not necessary to have knowledge of market niche providing you use certain affiliate marketing strategies (see later).

- ❖ Vendor should have good sales copy such as testimonials at minimum.
- ❖ Vendor should be able to respond to customer inquiries in timely manner to prevent refunds and chargebacks. Refunds and chargebacks lead to loss of affiliate commission.

In practice, it is difficult to find affiliate marketing programs and vendors who have all the characteristics mentioned here. You need to compare affiliate marketing programs and vendors and short list according to your preferences.

3   Best Products For Affiliate Marketing

Best products for affiliate marketing are as follows:

- ❖ Services that cannot be acquired for free online such as legal advice, tax consultancy, health care, insurance, horoscope, forex trading etc.

- Usually tangible goods cannot be acquired for free. However, it may not have higher commission percentage as compared to digital products or services. It does not mean that affiliate marketing programs such as offered by Amazon is not worthwhile.
- One to one or real time training programs.
- Digital products, such as ebook, audio/video, software etc. It includes educational materials movies, songs etc, which cannot be instantly downloaded and purchased at cheaper price than making visit to stores. Remember that those products can also be available for free online. Therefore, it must have USP (Unique Selling Point) to be able to make your visitors purchase using your referral.
- Goods or services which do not require physical interaction such as webhosting, credit card processing etc.
- Goods or services about which individual may not like to discuss publicly or face to face.

Step 3: AFFILIATE MARKETING STRATEGIES

Just as traditional marketing can be performed in countless number of ways; internet marketing can also be performed in countless number of ways. Affiliate marketing is a sub-category of internet marketing.

Your internet marketing strategy depends on the type of market niche in which you are operating and market segment to which you are trying to promote.

1   What is Market and Market Niche?

Market is the platform where buyers and sellers meet to buy or sell product.

Market niche is the sub division of market. Market niche can have its own sub market niches.

Example:

Internet marketing is sub niche of marketing. Internet marketing can have many market niche such as Affiliate marketing, PPC marketing, Blog Marketing etc.

Business can have market niche such as finance, accounting, marketing. Accounting can have further market niches such as financial accounting, management accounting, forensic accounting etc.

2   Market or Market Niche

Market in general is a broad term. Market refers to the place where buyer and seller meets to fulfill their objectives.

It is the sub market niche that is relevant for affiliate marketing. Affiliate marketer can choose as many market niches depending on skills, experience and resources available.

Focusing on market as whole or market niche depends on the level of resources and experience you have. For individuals and SMEs focus on market niche is a better choice.

Market niche can be sub divided into different categories such as by customer age, geo location, gender etc. see market segment later in this guide.

Example:

Affiliate Marketing Guide to Make Money Online can be offered to students, housewives and entrepreneurs.

It can be even further sub-divided geo location wise such as US, Europe and Asia.

More you closely identify your market niche, more targeted your affiliate marketing strategy will be. It will allow an affiliate to determine the demand and competition in particular market niche.

Identifying market niche allows you to obtain cross selling benefits. Marketing different product without any relationship among them does not provide any cross-selling benefits. Marketing closely related products enables you to sell more products to same customer and share resources such as domain name, software, processes, social networking accounts etc.

Identifying market niche also allows an affiliate to obtain economies of scale. You can negotiate bulk purchase discounts when purchasing articles, attract new vendors and other marketers to contact you for ventures.

Search engines like websites which is focused on particular market or market niche rather than many markets at the same time. Focusing on every market in general dilutes the density/importance of keywords of your website. Importance of keywords through the eyes of search engine can be seen in analytics tool provided by major search engines such as Google Analytics and Webmaster tools, Bing (MSN) Webmaster tools etc.

Focus on particular market niche allows affiliate to establish his/her authority as an expert. Therefore, referral made by an affiliate carries significant weight than referral made by an affiliate appearing as posting contents for hobby.

3   Selecting Market Niche

Consider, your prior knowledge and experience of internet marketing before you chose market niche and market segment. It is unlikely to find the market niche that is both profitable and feasible on the basis of skills and resources.

If you cannot find any market niche that is both profitable and feasible, go with the market niche that is feasible. It is because you are much likely face high competition in profitable niches and without having sufficient knowledge will reduce the likelihood of success. Even if you research the niche, it will take significant time to get started.

Example:

Affiliate might want to choose forex trading as market niche based on profitability but may lack necessary credentials, such as recognized relevant qualification, knowledge and experience, to make forex trading a feasible choice.

Choice of market niche is most critical part of your affiliate marketing career. Changing market niche is not possible without losing your existing marketing efforts and customer base.

You can either choose market niche based on your knowledge and experience or choose market niche entirely based on attractiveness of market niche.

Choosing market niche based on knowledge and experience may help an affiliate achieve above average profits in unattractive market.

Choosing market niche based on attractiveness may leave you earning below average or average profits. However, you may consider acquiring knowledge of particular market niche with the passage of time. You should consider the time available to learn new knowledge and combine profitability from existing job/business and affiliate marketing.

It is vital to find suitable market niche and target that niche rather than market in general. Affiliate should take care that your targeted market niche should not be too small to generate sufficient commission. On the other hand, if market niche you choose was too large, then it may have highly successful competitors and you may have a little chance to stand against those competitors.

If you are starting your career with no previous experience and knowledge such as in case you are a student or house wives having no work experience at all, then you may consider the attractiveness of market niche for the selection of market niche.

Market niche selection based on attractiveness is riskier than market niche selection based on knowledge and experience. Affiliate should take account of the level of risk he/she is prepared to accept.

Less profitable market niche may not have enough vendors to promote affiliate products. However, affiliate marketing strategy based on knowledge and skills allow an affiliate to become a vendor as well in the long term, which will allow him/her to ripe the benefits of having own product and avoid the limitations of affiliate marketing in the long term. See affiliate marketing for vendor later.

4 What is Market Segment?

Market segment is particular group of customers who share similar characteristics such as by age, sex, income, spending, levels country, occupation, education, risk attitude etc.

Difference between market niche and market segment is that market niche is by product and market segment is by people. First step is to choose product. Second step is to determine suitable group of people to promote product.

5 Market or Market Segment

Market segment identification allows you to write your promotional materials to target particular people of society. It will make your promotional materials standout from the rest of competition and perceived more relevant by the visitors.

Promotional materials closely identifying market segment will help to establish relationship and gain trust. Affiliate can be understood as a part of market segment.

Market segment allows you to choose suitable marketing strategy.

Example:

Affiliate having access to local people of the society due to large friend circle, professional relationship, social work etc. can choose offline marketing to bring visitor to his/her website; from where visitors may click on affiliate links.

Affiliate is promoting to young people, requires simple website design and easy means to follow up. Offering Newsletter subscription rather than RSS feeds (see later) may be more appropriate due to its simplicity.

6   Selecting Market Segment

If you are promoting products on self-help (market niche), then it can be promoted to many market-segments.

Example:

People want to improve themselves

People want to avoid pain and distress.

As discussed in context of market niche, it is vital to find suitable market segment and target that segment rather than market in general. Affiliate should take care that your targeted market segment should not be too small to generate sufficient commission. On the other hand, if market segment you choose was too large, then it may have highly successful competitors and you may have a little chance to stand against those competitors.

Size of the market segment should not be considered alone, choice of market segment should be based qualitative factors as well, such as ability to buy online, sophistication of customer, attitude towards buying new products, buying behavior (impulsive or considered), ethical viewpoints, such as wrongful chargebacks and refunds.

Market niche you have chosen also influence the choice of market segment.

Example:

Affiliate promoting products on betting/gaming may target wealthy (income) individuals.

7 Affiliate Marketing Strategies

Affiliate marketing strategies are techniques used to drive traffic (visitors) to vendor website. Affiliate marketing strategy chosen affects the quality, speed, cost, short term profitability, long term growth.

Below are some of the popular affiliate marketing techniques with pros and cons of each affiliate marketing technique. Choice of affiliate marketing technique depends on following factors:

- ❖ Communication skills,
- ❖ IT skills & resources (HTML, CSS, Web hosting),
- ❖ Knowledge of market niche,
- ❖ Effectiveness to bring targeted visitors,
- ❖ Control required over content structure and formatting,
- ❖ Maintaining ownership of contents,
- ❖ Time to generate earnings,

- ❖ Initial and subsequent costs,
- ❖ Ability to outsource or automate,
- ❖ Ability to carry out till foreseeable future,
- ❖ Measuring performance etc.

In addition, the type of visitors (existing or new) to which you want to market your products (see later).

You should divide some of the above-mentioned factors into primary and secondary factors.

Primary factors are those which cannot avoided in selection of internet marketing strategy. Which factors you consider as primary depends on your preferences.

Secondary factors are those which influence your preferences to adopt particular internet marketing strategy.

Strategies failing to meet primary requirements should be eliminated in selection process.

7.1 Free eBooks

Free eBook requires the knowledge of market niche. However, you can use PLR or public domain eBooks (see later) or hire an author to write an eBook for you. Similarly, PLR articles are also available. You can choose to compile PLR articles to create an eBook.

It is recommended that you rewrite PLR articles or ebook to increase its quality and make it look original work. Make sure that you have a right to modify or edit the contents.

Please note that PLR contents have different types of copyright rights allowed or restricted by the author. You need to carefully read the copyright notice.

Some of the copyrights are as follows

- Right to resell.
- Right to give it for free.
- Right to edit.

- Right to remove author attribution.

Above rights are not conclusive. There are many other rights exists.

Free eBook requires most time. However, you can hire freelancers from one of the many freelancing websites to rewrite or write contents for you from scratch. It is more authoritative as you will be considered as expert in the niche and legitimate person. Establishing authority is one of the persuasion techniques (see later). It will increase the likelihood of converting visitor into sale. Visitor will be already convinced by recommendations and referral of affiliate and regard affiliate referral as sign of quality for the product offered by vendor.

Free eBook can be used to promote the several related products at once such as listing useful resources. However, keeping too many links inside an eBook will make visitors feel like an advertisement brochure rather than informational ebook.

Free eBook depending upon the software used to compile can be used for viral marketing. Many eBook readers provide an option to share ebooks on social networking websites or just email.

Free eBooks does not necessarily require you to create and maintain your own website you can upload free eBook to online file sharing websites such as mediafire, 4shared etc. and ebook stores such as amazon, Scribd, SlideShare, Docstoc, Isuzu etc.

File sharing website only allow storing, downloading, sharing of files such as pdf, ppt, doc etc. Bookstores allow reading online; access other ebooks by same author, embedding, following ebook author, statistics etc. in addition to storing, downloading and sharing of files in different formats.

You can also make use of ebook aggregator or distributor to make your ebook listed at major ebook stores and manage all your ebooks from single place.

You can create your affiliate links inside ebooks. Online ebook stores also provide options for sharing and embedding of your eBook. If reader will share and other webmasters will embed your eBook, then it will create viral marketing effect.

To create viral marketing effect eBook should contain sufficient quantity and quality of information.

You can use URL shortening service (see later) to replace the affiliate link with user friendly link to avoid an eBook look like a promotional material.

eBooks can be theft by pirates. Therefore, it is necessary to secure your ebook (see later).

7.2 Email Marketing

Email marketing is the cheap way for promoting affiliate products. Email marketing is itself a separate internet marketing strategy, which requires skills, experience & resources to do it effectively.

Email marketing should be done carefully as there are legal requirements to comply with, in some jurisdictions, such as requirement to place unsubscribe link in emails, receiver must opt-in to receive emails etc.

Furthermore, shared web hosting providers have limitations on the number of emails sent per hour and per day. Violation of limits can result in suspension of web hosting account without prior notice. You must ask for details on email sending limits imposed by your web hosting provider.

Email marketing is useful to increase the earnings made per visitor. Affiliate can follow up visitors for new affiliate products.

Email marketing is not sending promotional contents every time. You need to provide them useful information as well. So that they can trust you and buy products from your referral.

You can send useful contents via articles inside email, link to article published on your blog. Providing links to your articles published on your blog is so useful SEO (see later). You can also provide newsletters or provide them free eBook.

Newsletters campaign can be run using PLR, public domain contents or you use can purchase article from freelance article writers.

Email marketing requires mailing list. Mailing list takes time to develop through legitimate means.

Email marketing requires offering free gifts/newsletters/email courses to induce visitor to subscribe to mailing list.

Other ways of doing email marketing is purchasing email list are:

- ❖ Getting email addresses from social networking account profiles and forum profiles,
- ❖ Getting email addresses using online web scrapping software,
- ❖ Sending undirected emails to domain names without knowing the user.

❖ Purchasing an email list from others.

Example:

Sending emails to info@accasupport.com or contact@accasupport.com. *As these email addresses are created by many websites*

These other ways of doing email marketing is not recommended.

Email marketing requires the use of email capturing software, auto responder software and mailing list management software.

Usually all these services can be obtained using single software or online services with more or less effectiveness depending on each software or online service. Select one which meets your all necessary requirements and cost budget.

Email marketing software are of two types.

❖ Server based (Online) email software

- ❖ Client based (locally installed on your device) email software

Some online services do not allow affiliate links inside email. However, you can place links to your website/blog.

Online services allow you to avoid undergo installation process and significant upfront payment for purchase of email marketing software. Online services may improve its interface on continuous basis and can be switched to different service provider, if your email marketing requirements changes or you are unsatisfied with their performance.

Server based email software can be accessed from anywhere such as at home or at work.

Server based email software is useful, if you use more than one computer such as at home and at work.

Server based email software allows you to send emails even when you switch off your computer.

Server based email software are more reliable, as they make backups of data on daily basis. In case of client-side email marketing software or one hosted with your webhosting service requires backup and protection of data by yourself.

Popular online services are aweber, mail chimp (free) etc. Free services like mail chimp provides free service but they also force their logos at the bottom of emails and provides limited features. Mail chimp does not allow affiliate links inside email.

PHPList is very popular free script for email marketing, which can be installed on your web hosting account. It can be installed using automatic script installers such as softaculous and fantastico that could be given in web hosting control panel. However, you can manually install just like other blogging and forum scripts.

Affiliates should not exclusively rely on email marketing. Email marketing can be used as complementary marketing strategy in combination with free ebooks, website or blogs.

7.3 Forums

Forums can be used to drive instant traffic. Forums require the use of communication skills. Forum postings should not look like advertisement. In that case, it will be removed by forum administrator and your account can be banned from using the forums. To avoid that read terms of service carefully.

Forums require the knowledge of market niche. As You will be answering to others issues or engaging in a discussion on topics for which little information is available on the web. Most people make postings on forums when they are not able to get help from anywhere else on the web. Therefore, it is highly likely that they buy recommended products to solve their problem or fulfill their information need.

Forums can be used with other affiliate marketing strategies such as blogging.

Using forums in combination with blog provides the following benefits.

- ❖ It helps to bring visitors to your website, where you can provide further information about the product.
- ❖ It helps preserving your affiliate marketing efforts. If vendor discontinues his/her product, then you can promote other similar products on blog or website.
- ❖ Links from Dofollow (see later) forums provide backlinks to your website. A polite way to place links is to use links in signature. Backlinks were the part of Google search engine algorithms, which is now of little importance due to later updates to the Google search engine algorithms.
- ❖ It provides opportunity to capture email addresses for subsequent follow up. You may drive visitors to your website and offer a free gift in return for contact information or an email address.

Affiliate may wish to establish his/her forums at his/her own website. There are many free scripts/softwares such as SMF, MyBB, phpBB etc which enables an affiliate to establish forums of professional quality.

Establishing own forums do not provide an affiliate with instant traffic (visitors). It could be argued that establishing its own forum will make affiliate using his/her resources and time promoting forums rather than promoting affiliate products.

However, establishing forums is long term investment which will make an affiliate earn above average profits than fellow affiliates in the long term.

7.4 Social Media Marketing

Social media marketing is a broad term. Many websites classified as social media website differs significantly in functionalities and policies.

Digg, StumbleUpon, Twitter, Facebook, delicious are significantly different in functionality (access to other users, text, images, videos, anchor text (see later), characters limit, Meta tags), scope (professional, entertainment) reach (general, invitation only) and targeted geo-location.

Social media websites are also known as social networking websites. However, social bookmarking websites are not social networking websites.

Social bookmarking websites are used by visitors to bookmark and manage their favorite websites. These social bookmarking websites provides advanced tools for managing bookmarks. Social bookmarking websites also provide other visitors with contents that are already liked or bookmarked by other visitors. People visit social bookmarking website to browse/search relevant information provided by high quality websites that is liked by other people. Therefore, referral from social bookmarking website carries higher weight for persuading visitors.

Social bookmarking does not require knowledge of market niche.

Social bookmarking provides instant traffic.

Social bookmarking can be automated or outsourced depending on your cost budget. Automating social bookmarking is the cheaper and better option.

Social media marketing is measurable which allows you to invest time and resources to social media website providing highest benefit. Social media websites provide analytical tools. It requires investing some time to use it effectively.

Social media websites work best with website/blog. Blogging software such as wordpress.org has many useful plugins that allow you to automatically post new and revised blog posts and pages to popular social networking sites.

7.5 Video Marketing

Video streaming sites allows you to upload and share videos. Some of the popular websites include youtube.com, metacafe.com, dailymotion.com etc. If website such as YouTube or any other which is blocked in your country, then you may consider using VPN or Proxy

Server (see later) to unblock these websites. Please note that visiting blocked sites using VPN or Proxy Server has legal consequences.

YouTube has an edge over other video streaming sites as it is the product of Google. Google frequently crawlers youtube.com for new contents and displays YouTube videos in search engine results.

These websites provide tools to upload videos and display affiliate links in the description box. You can use URL shortening service (see later) to save characters and hide your affiliate link.

Videos can enable an affiliate earn above average profits than affiliates that do not know video publishing or have tools such as camera, microphone, file format conversion tools, screen capturing software etc. Now days usage of smart phone is very common. You can use your smart phone to make a video.

You can annotate these videos such as creating subtitles for accessibility, using the free tools provided by video streaming websites.

Affiliate can use its contents placed on blog or inside eBook to create videos using screen capturing software.

Video marketing is useful in case affiliate product is in the form of CDs, DVDs or Video Downloads. These visitors have already preference for multimedia contents and prefer to purchase affiliate product from your referral than from other vendors offering eBooks or hard copies. Likewise, writing an ebook is useful when you are promoting an ebook.

7.6 Blogs/Websites

Blog/Websites provide more control over the content, format and structure. Affiliate marketer can convince the visitor and fill the gap identified in the sales copy of vendor.

Blog and website allow affiliate marketer to control the presentation of contents using HTML, CSS, JavaScript. It does not mean, if you don't know such as languages you cannot run a blog or website. However, knowing such as language will provide an edge over the competition. You can visit https://www.w3schools.com to learn these languages free of cost.

Many blogging platforms allow free blogs hosting on their sub-domain. You can purchase your own domain name to create authority over visitors, make your blog/website look more professional and obtain long term SEO (search engine optimization) benefits. You can host your blog/website using your own domain on free blogging platforms such as blogger.

Blog/Website is an essential part of affiliate marketing particularly, if you want to pursue affiliate marketing as your career rather than one off project to achieve particular goal such as repairing debt.

Blogs/websites are not quick source of earnings. It could be argued that time and resource spent on promoting blog/website could be used to promote affiliate products and establishing blog/website increases the efforts required to earn commission. However, they can provide long term earnings till foreseeable future.

Blogs/websites helps to avoid the risk of loss of affiliate marketing effort due to discontinuation of affiliate program or banning you. You can send your loyal visitors to promote affiliate products at other affiliate programs.

Blogs/websites helps coordinating different internet marketing strategies such as email marketing and offline marketing.

Blog/websites do not generate traffic on its own. You need to adopt other internet marketing strategies to promote your blog post or page. These internet marketing strategies include paid advertisements, social networking/media marketing, existing mailing list and so on.

One of the internet marketing strategy worth mentioning is SEO.

7.7 SEO (Search Engine Optimization)

Search Engines are among the most popular means of surfing over the internet. Getting high ranking in search engine results is essential to get free and highly relevant/targeted traffic that will be interest in your product.

Google is the market leader in search engine. Google has 90% market share in the world. Bing is the next most popular search engine.

Getting ranked higher in search engine ranking is not easy. It takes time and consistently good performance (uptime, errors, speed, bounce rate etc.) to get higher rank in search engines. Each website is competing against each other to ranked higher. Furthermore, search engines change their algorithms over time to improve search engine results quality.

If you do not know that technicalities involved in doing SEO. You can outsource it to SEO solution provider. Remember that both white hat and black hat SEO practices exists. If your SEO solution provider is involved in black hat SEO practice. You have a risk of getting removed from search engine index or listing.

7.8 Article Marketing

Article marketing can be used for affiliate marketing purpose. Affiliate can submit articles to third party website rather than publishing articles to your own blog/website.

Article marketing allows affiliates to make use of core knowledge of market niche and avoid technical difficulties involved in creating and managing blog/websites. Article directory websites market your articles and also allow affiliates to monetize articles using selected advertising programs. Article marketing is effectively an internet marketing strategy to make money online.

Article marketing may not be possible using PLR articles and public domain materials. PLR articles and public domain materials may be already published by other webmasters. Article directories require original and good quantity and quality content as they spent their money in promoting these articles. You may consider rewriting original articles to make it unique. Many article spinners such as spinchimp (free) can be used for this purpose.

Affiliate may consider using freelance article writers to create articles for article marketing purpose. Articles need to be evaluated for keyword density (relevance), article length (quantity), number of different points discussed (quality) etc. Affiliate can check articles for duplicate contents before making payment. One service I know is copyscape.com (free). You can also copy / paste a sentence or paragraph in Google web search to check for duplicate content.

Article directories also allow affiliates to place certain number of links in an article. Affiliates can place their affiliate links or link to their website or blog.

Each article directories have its own terms and conditions, which an affiliate must read to avoid getting disapproved and fitness of using article directory for affiliate marketing purpose.

Popular article directories are hubpages, squidoo, ezinearticles, ehow, about.com. It also allows you to create and edit your articles using their online HTML editor. Some of the frequently used HTML tags are discussed later in the ebook.

7.9 RSS Feeds

RSS Feeds provide automatic updates to subscribers whenever you publish new contents to your blog/website.

It requires that you have your own blog/website. Most blogging platforms have RSS Feeds enabled such as blogger.com. In other cases, websites have to manually create RSS Feeds.

Understanding and using RSS Feeds is extremely complex process. It also requires skills and experience of using RSS Feeds on the part of visitors. Therefore, it is not suitable for targeting inexperienced users.

7.10 Paid Advertising

Most paid advertising program requires you to pay per click. You will only incur cost when visitor will click on your placed link in an advertisement. On the other hand, some advertising program require you to pay fixed sum of money for a particular period of time.

Now days all major search engines and social media websites such as Google, Bing and Facebook respectively do not allow affiliates to place their affiliate links. However, you can place links to your blog or website. Where you can presell visitors, capture email address etc. before sending it to vendor website.

Search engines such as Google and Bing have both paid listing in search engine ranking results and publisher network. In search engine results your advertising will be place at high position depending on your bid (cost per click). Publisher network is the network of blogs/websites partnered with such advertising programs to make money by showing ads on the blog/website.

Getting accepted in search engine paid listing can bring you highly relevant traffic who already have preference for the product you are promoting and your blog/website will be perceived as of high quality as you have gone through the vigorous approval process by these advertisement program providers.

To get approved your ads in advertisement programs, your content must provide real value to visitors and comply with their terms of services. Please carefully read their terms of service before applying for running your ads. Compliance with their terms of service and quality standard will both reduce the cost of advertising and avoid you from being removed from their program. Also read the guidelines and tips made available by advertising network to make use of resources provided by advertising network to its fullest.

Paid advertising can provide you with instant traffic and take off much of the activities involved in internet marketing. However, paid advertising if not used effectively or affiliate product which you are promoting is not attractive enough, then it can lead to monetary losses.

Paid advertising is only recommended for affiliate products already tested for its ability to convert visitor into sale. Affiliate products should be tested using free ways of affiliate marketing. Or may set a small marketing campaign no more than $10 to determine the conversion rate of affiliate product.

Conversion rate is a key factor in determining which affiliate product to promote. Higher the conversion rate more profit you will earn. Bring visitors to your blog/website or sending them to vendor website requires time and money. Higher conversion rate means more visitors are ending up buying the affiliate product out of total number of visitors.

Paid advertising requires the understanding of analytical information provided by advertising program. Misinterpretation of analytical information can result in monetary losses.

Example:

Large number of searches does not necessarily mean large number of customers. Majority of visitors can be from locations which have very poor history of online shopping.

Affiliate marketing eBooks may have higher number of searches than affiliate marketing guide. However, affiliate marketing eBooks may be searched by visitors having poor history of online shopping. While affiliate marketing guide may be searched by visitors have excellent history of online shopping.

Wrong selection of keywords may provide an affiliate with large number of visitors. But it may not convert enough visitors to breakeven. Higher the cost per click, higher conversion rate for particular affiliate product will be required to breakeven (no profit/no loss).

Lack of knowledge on demand for affiliate product in different geo-locations and technical jargons used to search over the web can lead to losses.

It would be better to set large number of marketing campaigns with lower cost per click to spread the risk of wrong keyword selection and reduce sales volume required to breakeven (no profit/ no loss). Each campaign should focus on different market segment so that you can direct your resources to best performing campaigns and withdraw loss making campaigns.

Paid advertising will turn affiliate marketing from knowledge intensive business to finance intensive business. Profits are related to amount of advertisement made rather than related to internet marketing skills. However, you need to have good analytical and mathematical skills to make profit from paid advertisements.

Keywords selected (including negative keywords such as free, without, no etc.) to target relevant visitors at each stage of purchase cycle (see later) also affect the conversion rate.

If paid advertising is used, it is recommended that affiliate set an upper limit to campaign budget to limit the risk of losses.

Paid advertising programs such as Google AdWords do not allow selection of some keywords.

I will advise you not to spend the amount of money on paid advertising that you cannot afford to lose.

8 Matching Internet Marketing Strategy with Affiliate Product

Matching means consistency between the type of products and internet marketing strategy. If you are promoting eBooks then creating eBooks are the best option; because it will directly attract visitors interested in reading eBooks.

If you are promoting membership website, then forums and social networking websites would be the best.

If you are selling audio/video, then video marketing would be the best option.

There is no one best option that suits all type of products, market niche & market segments.

What is best affiliate marketing strategy depend on the type of product you are promoting and depends on the people to which you are promoting. However, choosing the best affiliate strategy for your market niche or product type (eBooks, Videos, Shippable) is not sufficient to bring intended results. You need to excel at relevant affiliate marketing strategy and need resources to carry out such affiliate marketing strategy.

Example:

Forums will not benefit you if you cannot actively participate in forums due to other commitments.

Using paid advertisement will not lead to required results if you do not have depth of knowledge of keywords and tools provided by advertising program.

9   New Visitors or Existing Visitors

It depends on the following factors.

9.1 Cost

New visitors require time and cost particularly if you are using paid advertising such as PPC (pay per click) advertising.

Existing visitors do not require advertisement expenditure. Retaining the existing visitors will improve your Return on Investment (ROI). That is why, email marketing is so essential to retain existing visitors.

9.2 Market niche

If your market niche, such as education or health care, has certain customer life cycle, then you have to actively seek new visitors. Visitors will lose interest once they have achieved certain qualification or remedy respectively.

If your market niche is of innovative nature which renders the existing goods obsolete such as movies, Story Books, Games etc., then you may keep your existing visitors interested by offering new products.

9.3 Existing Strategies

If you are using affiliate marketing in combination with paid advertising such as Google AdSense as monetization strategy, then new visitors would maximize the combine profitability. Google AdSense requires new visitors, as advertisements may remain same over time.

Advertisers usually require new visitors rather existing visitors. Therefore, you need visitors which are unfamiliar with the advertisements on your webpage. Sponsors have usually interest in number of unique visits rather total number of visits.

However, if you are selling your own products as well as affiliate products, then existing visitor would maximize your combine profitability. You can follow up your existing customers to promote affiliate products to them.

9.4 Access to Affiliate Programs

If you are living in a country which has fewer options for receiving payment or transaction cost of receiving payment are high or few marketplaces supporting your country. It will limit your access to number of affiliate products suitable to your needs. In that case, promoting existing products to new visitors would be a better option.

9.5 Market size

If market niche of your affiliate products has small market size (number of potential customers), then marketing to existing visitors would be a better option.

9.6 Risk

Existing vendors who has already brought from your referral are more like to purchase again. Existing visitors are less risky as their integrity has already been known. New visitors may exploit refund policies to get access to the products for free especially in case of digital goods. In case of refunds both vendor and affiliate have to lose profit from a sale.

10 Know Your Customer

Knowledge of buying behavior, taste, fashion, values and beliefs of your targeted customer is of prime importance to persuade customers to buy product.

If you promote a product in the way that is unethical to customers in particular niche. For example, sending unsolicited emails for selling replica products would be acceptable to visitors in some countries. However, it would not be appreciated by visitors in other countries.

Young age visitors such as students may not have higher spending capability. However, middle age people such as business or salaried person have higher spending capability.

Education and level of sophistication of visitors also influence how they respond to your marketing campaigns.

Motive or requirements of customer behind buying the product is important.

It can be questioned when selecting affiliate products for promotion that vendor has any USP (unique selling point) in order to meet customer requirements to motive.

11 Purchase Cycle/Buying Funnel

Purchase cycle refers to the process through which customer passes in making buying decision. Purchase cycle involve stages from getting familiar with generic product to after sales review.

Purchase cycle has influence over marketing strategy and likelihood of making sales.

Following are the stages involved in purchase cycle.

11.1 Awareness

Customer gets familiar with generic product. Customer has only listened about the product but not have any knowledge regarding the product.

Example:

Customer may have listened about the smart phone but may do know what the smart phone is.

11.2 Knowledge

Customer acquires the knowledge about the generic product.

Example:

Customer gets knowledge that it is a pocket-sized phone capable to connect to internet.

11.3 Interest

Customer develops interest in the product.

Example:

Customer finds the smart phone relevant to his/her needs and want to try it.

Interest can be developed by describing the benefits associated with products.

Benefits can be financial as well as non-financial.

Financial benefits are more likely to motivate customers. Financial benefits can be reliably estimated by customers.

Non-financial benefits are quantitative and qualitative such as improved social status, independence, confidence etc.

11.4 Introduction

Customer came to know about the vendor.

Example:

Customer knew about the smart phone supplier such as Samsung.

Customer may also visit other vendors such as Samsung, Motorola, Apple etc. during the online shopping.

It is the job of affiliate marketer to introduce visitor to vendor.

11.5 Preference

Customer prefers products offered by particular vendor than other vendors offering the same product.

Example:

Customer felt that smart phone manufactured by Samsung have better camera than other suppliers.

Preference can be developed by providing free gifts, customer loyalty discounts, early bird discounts, bulk purchase discounts etc.

Affiliate marketers can persuade customers to buy vendor product by offering free eBooks, if they purchase from your reference.

11.6 Purchase

Customer makes the purchase.

Example:

Customer buys the smart phone at Samsung website.

11.7 Review

Customer reviews the purchase decision.

Example:

Customer receives feedback from his/her friends and relatives on the performance and price of smart phone.

Customer decides course of action for next purchase that is whether to buy newer models from Samsung or choose other supplier next time.

Customer may also review by comparing product quality and price offered by other vendors and comparing the product quality with price of the purchased product.

12 Implications of Purchase Cycle for Keyword Selection

Customer at later stages of purchase cycle is more likely to buy and requires fewer marketing efforts and cost.

Customer already know about the vendor product more likely to purchase than customer who have only awareness of the product. Affiliate marketer has to create preference for affiliate products such as by writing review, list of affiliate products intended to provide the same benefits.

Example:

Writing review for a webhosting provider or providing list of best, top, most, popular web hosting providers.

It implies that existing customer is more likely to buy providing that he/she is satisfied with former purchase.

Relevant keywords for customers at knowledge stage are number of benefits, number of reasons, Why to etc.

Relevant keywords for customers at awareness stage is what, how, when, who, etc. However, for affiliate marketing purpose what and how are the useful keywords in most cases. When and Who could be for limited time content such as news and stories, which have limited life. However, if you discuss any hot news of your market niche earlier than other publishers, then you may get high number of visitors in the short term who may buy affiliate products. News can be good for making money online through participating in advertisements programs such as Google AdSense.

Step 4: CREATING PROMOTIONAL MATERIALS

1 Choosing Keywords For Promotional Materials

Choosing the keywords depends on:

1.1 Customer You Want To Target

Customer in different geo location may use different jargon for same information. Large number of searches does not necessarily mean high quality keyword. Keywords having large number of searches may be related to geo-location having few buyers.

Developing countries with high population amounts to significant proportion of global searches. However, visitors may not have facility (debit/credit cards, country not supported by payment processor) to purchase online or visitors may buy the same product locally at much lower cost or visitors may be using internet as a source of free information.

Example:

Customer may use the internet to select the vendor for buying smart phone. However, he/she may prefer to buy it locally by inspecting its performance, enjoying shopping with friend or relatives, buy from local retailer at cheaper cost due to market segmentation pricing by vendor.

In case of digital products, visitors may be looking for free products. Visitors may use the keyword 'free' in his/her search query. Therefore, using negative keywords such as free, without, NO etc. in Google AdWords and Bing Advertisement will eliminate visitors who have does not commercial intent. Thus, reducing the cost of advertisement and increase conversion rate.

1.2   Marketing Budget or Time

Keywords chosen depend on marketing budget you have. If you have very large marketing budget (time or resources), then you may consider targeting customer at knowledge stage of purchase cycle. However, if you have small budget, then you may consider targeting customer at purchase stage of purchase cycle. Visitor using the keyword such as buy is an indication of commercial intent.

Please note that customers at earlier stages of purchase cycle are riskier than customers at later stages of purchase cycle.

Customers at earlier stages may not lead to enough conversion rate (% visitors converted into sale) to make marketing worthwhile on financial grounds.

1.3   Stage Of Market Life Cycle

In growing market niche, such as make money online, keywords at earlier stages of purchase cycle will lead to more visitors.

If market niche is at maturity stage, then targeting visitors at awareness or knowledge at would not much benefit. Customers are already familiar with the product and its benefits. Most of them are likely to be repeat purchasers; therefore, using keywords for visitors at later stages of purchase cycle are much better.

1.4 Return on Investment

Affiliate marketer may want to earn certain amount of money over definite period. Some keywords may make you earn $10,000 by investing $8,000 than other keywords making you earning $1,000 by investing $50 in 1 month time. Earning $1,000 by investing $50 will provide much higher ROI than earning $10,000 by investing $8,000. However, focusing only high ROI keywords may not meet your financial objectives. Therefore, quality of keywords that attract highly relevant visitors should your first priority in order to increase ROI. However, volume of searches related to the keyword should also be taken into account to make sure to get sufficient visitors to make enough sales.

1.5 Affiliate Marketing Strategy Adopted

If you have adopted Search Engine Optimization (SEO) strategy, then you should choose keywords based on searches made by customers for creating the content. However, if you are using Social Media Optimization (SMO) strategy, then you may use keywords which are closely related to affiliate product. Using keywords based on searches made by customers may not be much relevant for promoting the affiliate product or may lead to targeting wrong keywords. Ideally, you should choose keywords that are relevant to your affiliate product and then filter all relevant keywords for number of searches made by customers.

2   Keywords Selection for Search Engine Optimization

Length, density and combination of keywords chosen impacts your search engine ranking.

Example:

Affiliate Marketing Guide

Affiliate Marketing Ebook to Make Money Online from Home

Both of the above has different keywords length, density and combination.

The former one has high keyword density for visitor searching for affiliate marketing and the later one low keyword density for visitor searching the same.

Combination of one or two keywords can result in large number of searches in keywords tool. On the other hand, combination of three or four can result in considerably small number of searches.

If you choose short phrases, then you will be competing with large number of publishers those who have chosen short phrases as well as those who have chosen lengthy phrases for which your chosen short phrase is part of lengthy phrases.

If you chose lengthy phrases, you will automatically be ranked in search engine results for short search queries.

Ideally, keywords chosen should be three to four words long to both ensure you are getting or paying for relevant visitors only and attract sufficient number of visitors.

Just choosing the right length of keywords is not enough. Individual keywords chosen should have close relationship with each other.

One way to choose the right combination of keywords is to relate topic and its purpose or benefit.

Ideally, choose the combination of keywords that are of sufficient length and have sufficient number of searches in particular combination.

In addition, you should make sure that the combination of keywords is consistently used by visitors over time and are not subject to one off incident.

You should determine the number of publishers gets ranked for particular combination of keywords. Competition percentage given in keywords tools provided by advertisement programs such as Google AdWords is not relevant for this purpose. Competition shows that how many websites are using paid advertising for particular keywords combination.

You should type the keywords combination in search engine for which you want to optimize your webpage. In most search engines, you will see number of results directly below the search box.

Keywords combination having higher number of searches to number of publisher ratio should be ranked first.

Keywords/Publisher Ratio = Number Of Searches/Number Of Publishers

Care should be taken that chosen keywords needs to be relevant to your affiliate product or market niche.

Bringing visitors to your website or blog will not earn you money, if visitors are not interested in products you are promoting. It would be better to have small but highly targeted visitors. Highly targeted visitors mean that those who are at later stages of purchase cycle and have commercial intent.

Strength of highest ranked publisher should also be taken into account. Keywords combination having large number of publishers but publishers relevant to those keywords may have scope for improvement in their websites/blogs for search engine optimization, which an affiliate can use to achieve higher ranking.

Checking strength of publishers also provides you important competitor information. You can visit highly ranked websites to understand their usage of keywords density, loading time, quality of content (text, graphics, videos), quantity of content, useful plugins used by them, marketing strategies, useful keywords etc. Use view source command in your browser using context menu to get in-depth information.

3   Persuasive Copywriting

The following points should be noted when writing promotional content.

Providing advantages as well as some disadvantages. Disadvantages will enhance the value of advantages and make your article or review as providing unbiased information.

Telling how benefits from buying a particular product exceed cost. Benefit can be financial as well as non-financial such as improved self-esteem, freedom etc. Higher the benefits compared to cost more likely visitor is going to buy the product.

Providing comparison of product features with other products intended to provide same benefits to create preference for affiliate product.

Providing testimonials to give evidence of intended benefits of the affiliate product from viewpoint of other customers. People are more likely to buy if other customers are satisfied from the use of product. Testimonials need to be genuine; otherwise it may result in violation of terms of service of affiliate program and sanctions can be imposed by local law.

Make them understand that you know the requirements of your visitors. Tell the story of your personal experience with the affiliate product or generic product.

Do not write something that your customers may not agree with. Making your customers disagree with your opinion reduces the chances of making sale.

Provide answer to questions that a potential customer could ask during the purchase cycle. As an affiliate you can make up the deficiencies identified in sales copy of an affiliate product written by vendor.

Provide them with free knowledge to gain their confidence on the expected benefits from the recommended affiliate product. Providing free knowledge will provide satisfaction to visitors that you know the market niche well and are able to provide good solutions.

Make easy for them to ask questions and receive replies.

4   Best Content for Affiliate Marketing

Affiliate marketing is about providing awareness, knowledge, introducing and creating preference for affiliate products. Affiliate marketer can choose to create its own sales copy based on evaluation of affiliate products or weakness identified in vendor sales copy. In any case, do not make statements that are opposite to vendor's sales copy, refund policy, terms of service etc. It will upset your visitor and perceive your referral and vendor as scam.

4.1 Reviews

Writing review is one of the most popular methods for affiliate marketing. Review should provide answers to the questions and benefits expected by the customers from the use of vendor product.

Visitor looking for review would have interest in generic product and want to find the best vendor for that generic product. Or

Visitor has already visited to vendor website and wants assurance from independent party on the quality of vendor products.

Reviews target customers at later stages of purchase cycle. Therefore, reviews are more likely to convert customer into sale.

Important point to keep in mind while writing review is that your review should not look biased. It should explain both pros and cons of affiliate products. Explaining some limitations will provide significance to benefits associated with the product. Without limitations your review will look as a sales page.

Ideally, you should never promote those affiliate products to which you are not satisfied by yourself. Promoting low quality products will lead to loss of visitors and they will not ever click on your website next time in the search engine results.

For long term affiliate marketing success, affiliate should introduce its visitors to suitable affiliate products using his/her knowledge of the market niche.

If you are writing reviews, then you can create rating systems using widgets to make your review look more professional. Many content management systems and blogging software such as Joomla and wordpress.org respectively has free plugins (widgets) that you can use for this purpose. Many of these plugins allow you to artificially set number of votes and rating.

4.2 Product Price Comparisons

You can provide comparison of several affiliate products at once. It will increase the chances of conversion of visitor into sales. If a visitor does not like one vendor product than he/she can may end up buying other vendor product. In all cases, you will end up with earning commission providing the visitor has an intention to buy online.

Example:

Top Ten List

Best Products List

However, you may have to sign up to more than one affiliate programs/marketplaces and monitor your accounts for timely payments and communications such as revision in terms of service, commission, payment methods and payout threshold etc.

This kind of strategy works well with digital products such as software, membership websites as well as shippable goods such as mobile phones, laptops etc.

Tip:

Amazon affiliate program is a good place to promote both digital and shippable goods. It has good conversion rate on average 10%. However, it is lower commission percentage than affiliate programs such as click2sell which offers mostly digital products.

4.3 Lists

You can provide list of top, most, best products in your niche containing both free and affiliate products. Visitors looking for high quality services may prefer to purchase paid services. Be careful that your views should not be perceived as biased. Affiliate should really include thoroughly researched contents.

You can search over the internet for quantity and quality of free resources available as a substitute for affiliate product. If there were many high-quality free resources are available to get the same benefits as offered by affiliate product, then affiliate marketer should really reconsider his/her decision to promote the affiliate product.

Contents in the form of lists are liked by most visitors and shared on social networking websites. Lists are easy to navigate for relevant information and attract people considering time as money.

Lists are particularly liked by major search engines and it tend to rank well in search engines.

4.4 Problem Solving

You can create articles on no. of ways to, how to topics. Where you can provide links to different affiliate products designed to provide the solution to same problem. In addition, you should include some free ways of doing things to create perception of informational contents rather than promotional material.

Visitors may be searching for free information to get their problem solved. Problem solving articles target visitors at earlier stages (knowledge) of purchase cycle. Therefore, it may target large number of customers but likelihood conversion of these visitors into sale is lower.

You can create article explaining how to do particular task using affiliate product. These kinds of articles are particularly useful for promoting software and online services such as payment processing, do it yourself guides etc.

5 Obtaining Promotional Contents

5.1 PLR

PLR (Private Label Rights) articles/ebooks are a good way for getting promotional contents. Private label rights contents are also subject to copyright restrictions. Private label rights mean that you can use your own name as creator of materials or remove copyright attribution from the material. It does not necessarily mean that you can provide it as a free gift or create ebook to sell. PLR contents are copyright protected unless copyright owner has explicitly granted certain rights to user (see earlier).

PLR articles can be used for email marketing purpose, blog post, social networking purpose etc. However, if you want to use it for SEO purpose, then you must rewrite it using different jargons, including images (new or resizing existing images, alt text, caption, link title) , changing structure of sentence (active or passive voice), body (paragraph or list) and formatting (headings, bold, italics) to make it original. Search engine likes only unique contents, which was not published by any other website.

IMPORTANT: *Do not copy/paste your content from your website to Social Media Marketing Website and Forums etc. Search engines will consider your original content as duplicate and penalize you in search engine ranking.*

Many softwares available online for free, which allows you to rewrite articles. Usually these are known as content spinners or article rewriters. However, quality of content rewritten by these softwares may not exactly the same as manually rewritten content. Content spinners are useful where you want to rewrite the same articles many times. Free versions are usually limited to particular times while full versions are more functional and have high rewriting capability.

PLR articles would have published by large number of websites not having SEO strategy. These websites will be indexed by search engines but they do not rely on getting traffic (visitors) from search engines rather they drive traffic by engaging existing and referrals from existing visitors, social media etc.

5.2 Public Domain Materials

Copyright materials which lost their copyright protection entitlement are in public domain. In addition, materials published earlier than 1923 A.D are now in public domain. However, materials published later than 1923 A.D can also be in public domain due to several reasons, such as failure to renew copyright license, author donated the material to public domain, death of author not having successors to claim ownership of copyright materials, non-renewal of copyright protected materials due to short economic life such as movies, cartoons, games etc. In addition, work of government officials resulted as a part of their duties are also public domain materials.

Please note that all free materials available publicly are not in public domain regardless of copyright notice given in the material or not. By default, every original and fixed (documented, recorded) work is copyright protected from the time it is fixed even if it is never published.

Copyright infringement involves publication of materials subject to copyright even if you earn no financial benefits at all.

Using materials for affiliate marketing purpose are not exempted from copyright infringement under fair usage policy.

Materials used for educational purpose are exempt from copyright infringement.

One backup copy created of material to restore it later in case of loss or damage is exempt from copyright infringement.

Using copyright materials on your blog or website may lead to termination of your web hosting account or removal from social networking websites, removal from search engine index etc. In addition, affiliate marketplace may ban you from promoting affiliate products to preserve the reputation of vendors and marketplace itself.

You need to thoroughly read the terms of service. Selling of public domain materials such as book are restricted by some websites.

Example:

Selling public domain ebooks are prohibited by almost all online ebook stores, such as Amazon for example.

6 Securing Contents from Theft

Content theft is major problem in internet marketing. To attract visitors, your content must be accessible to search engines and easily accessible to visitors. Protecting your contents (ebooks or website) with user passwords limits to visibility of contents. Search engines cannot index those contents; which user cannot access freely.

Useful contents in the form of images lead to the same effect. Search engine uses text to rank contents. Images are not readable by search engines. Contents inside image can be communicated through defining alt or alternative tag. However, now days search engines are attempting to read text into images using OCR. You can also show captions with your images to define your content to search engines and visitors.

Fortunately, there are some ways, which lets an affiliate protect his/her contents to some extent without limiting access to content. However, none of these methods are 100% effective.

PDF is among the commonly used format for sharing contents online. You can add meta tags such as title, description, author name, comments to optimize your PDF for search engines. Many PDF readers let publisher do disabling printing, copy/paste, annotations, modification, editing etc. in PDF. Owner can encrypt PDF ebook with owner password to prevent piracy. Do not lock your content with user password if you want to share your contents publicly. Many online eBook stores do not allow files secured with user password.

eBooks in PDF format can also contain JavaScript to protect your content. You can set the limits on number of times a user can open the pdf file or set the time period after which pdf files cannot be open.

To protect website, many online services and plugins exists that lets you to display embed dialog box when someone tries to copy contents from your blog/website. You can also disable right click to prevent others view your source code.

Another free service enables to monitor contents for piracy is copyscape.com. Affiliate can copy/paste the contents he/she wants to check for piracy and It also helps determining duplicate contents on internal webpages and other websites.

If affiliate will have duplicate contents on his/her own website, then search engines will choose to display the webpage based its own algorithms. Therefore, affiliate can check the contents for duplication and adopt the following strategies as appropriate.

Rewrite duplicate contents or add additional content such as images, videos and text to make it significantly different.

- ❖ Combine pages having almost same content into one webpage.
- ❖ Provide **canonical** Meta tag into web page header. If you are using blog such as wordpress.org, then you can use plugin to insert canonical Meta tag.

HTML for canonical meta tag is:

```
<link rel="canonical" href="http://example.com/page.html"/>
```

Provide link to main webpage on all duplicate webpages indicates search engine the address of original webpage. Search engine will simply ignore the webpages having canonical Meta tag in search engine results.

Step 5:
BOOSTING AFFILIATE MARKETING

1 **Productivity Tools and Techniques**

1.1 **URL Shortners**

URL shortners can be used to hide your affiliate link. Social networking site usually do not allow anchor text using HTML to create links rather your link will be displayed as follows http://affiliatelink.vendor.affiliateprogram.com

Using the link as above looks ugly and takes significant number of characters. Social networking sites, such as twitter allows very limit characters to show in its posts. Therefore, URL shortners can save your plenty of space so that you can use it more wisely.

URL shortners can be used to display the link of your choice based on the keywords and length of URL you want.

There are many third-party websites which offers free URL shortening services online such as Tinyurl, bit.ly etc.

However, using these URL shortening service can be perceived as spammy as their domain names are not meaningful and visitors may have seen URL placed over the internet many times. In addition, the keywords you want to use may have already be taken.

Solution to these problems is installing your own URL shortening software. One of the free software I personally use is Yourls. Yourls is 100% free URL shortening software.

Yourls can be used to replace your affiliate link with URL which visitor may like to visit by avoiding the perception of promotion materials inferred from original affiliate link.

You can also share your shortened link to popular social networking sites, such as Facebook, Twitter etc.

In addition, Yourls has statistics feature to track short links for source of visitor and number of visitors; to enable affiliate measure the effectiveness of particular internet marketing strategy. Affiliate may consider creating separate short link for each internet marketing strategy.

Yourls is hosted on your own web hosting account. Therefore, it does not bear the risk of discontinuity of URL shortening service and getting banned from using their services.

Yourls software compulsorily requires a web hosting account which has PHP and MySQL database features. Usually, all web hosting providers have these fundamental features.

Yourls can be installed using automatic script installers such as softaculous and fantastico.

1.2 Auto Responders

Autoresponder software enables scheduling of email messages. Autoresponder varies in functionality. Autoresponders are of two types

Simple auto responders only allow sending emails at pre-determined point in time. More sophisticated autoresponders also allow setting intervals between emails, number of emails, start and end time.

Simple autoresponders are usually provided inside web hosting control panel such as cPanel. Sophisticated autoresponders such as infinite responder is free to download. However, if you need high quality autoresponders to automate all activities related to email marketing, run multiple email campaign at once, then you may consider a paid one, such as aweber, mail chimp etc.

1.3   Auto Poster Plugins

Wordpress.org blogs have free auto poster plugins. It allows affiliate to automatically submit posts to social networking and other popular blogging platforms. This plugin saves plenty of time required to manually share your posts on many social networking websites.

1.4   Automatic Social Submitter

Automatic social submitter can be used if you want to submit your contents to wider social networking sites.

Some online platform provides free social submission services such as socialmarker.com, seesmic.com, socialadr.com, onlywire.com etc.

Above auto social bookmarking website have both free and paid programs. You can start with free program as your requirements get increase you can switch to paid softwares.

Free services and softwares are effectively semi-automatic rather than fully automatic. Semi-automatic services and softwares reduce the time taken to complete tasks manually.

2   Outsource or Automate

In an affiliate marketing career, you will find certain task that you cannot be it yourself. It is the time for seeking expert help. Tasks such as designing website theme and graphics designing should be outsourced.

Activities of repetitive nature such as email marketing would be automated to save time.

To be a successful affiliate marketer, do not attempt to do everything by yourself. Get expert help and invest your money in useful tools.

Just focusing on core activities such as selecting affiliate products for promotion, selecting affiliate marketing strategies will increase the likelihood of success than if you are trying to do everything by yourself.

3 Common Mistakes Made by Affiliate Marketers

3.1 Not Creating his/her Own Blog/Website

Creating your own blogs helps you establish authority over visitors. You would be recognized as an expert providing useful information.

Blogs/Website helps you implement other internet marketing strategy; such as email marketing. Blog/Website serves as central hub which connects and complements other internet marketing strategies.

Blogs helps you to preserve your affiliate marketing efforts. Instead of providing contents to third party websites, you can place those contents to your own blog. You can then share these contents via social media, forums, emails to bring visitors to your blog where you can presell those visitors before sending them to affiliate product landing page.

If you place contents on third-party website such as forums, article directories, then they become the owner of the content. Blog helps affiliate to retain ownership of contents. Even, if they allow you to remove contents, instead removal from search engine index takes time. To publish your content as unique content you need to wait till removal from search engine index. It is also not viable to manual remove all contents place at different websites.

Blogs are your property which can be sold to realize cash. Value of blog depends on the number of visitors, market niche, revenue generation, statistical information available to prove your claims. Contents on affiliate blog can also be compiled and sold as an eBook later in your career.

3.2   Not Capturing Email Addresses

Capturing email addresses will not cost you any money. Even, if you cannot provide free ebook, software, videos etc., then you can offer newsletter subscription in which you can provide links to useful and relevant contents such as ebooks, articles, videos etc. published over the web.

If you are using content management system or blogs, then you can easily get newsletter plugin from your content management system or blogging software community such as joomla and WordPress respectively.

4   Not Choosing Suitable Software for Web Design

Please note that content management system is not the same as blogging software. Content management systems are usually more sophisticated and do not indexed by blog search engines. While blogs created by blogging software such as wordpress.org get indexed in blog search engines. Content management systems provide substitute to HTML websites rather than blog. If you are an affiliate marketer than blogging software would be a better choice.

Blogging software has the ability to reach wide spread audience than content management system and HTML websites. Blogging softwares automatically create feeds, which have to be created manually using XML in case of HTML websites.

Plugins available for blogging software such as WordPress makes it ideal for affiliate marketing.

Blogs are frequently indexed by search engines than websites. The primary purpose of blogs is to enable interaction between publishers & visitors and between visitor & visitors.

Front end features are those affecting browsing experience.

Back end features are those affecting administration of software.

Following are some of the feature against you would evaluate the software.

- ❖ Ability to migrate to different web host.
- ❖ Uptime of web site.
- ❖ Ability to migrate to different software.
- ❖ Future updates and support from supplier.

- ❖ Availability of required plugins.
- ❖ Free plugins available.
- ❖ Security features provided by supplier.
- ❖ Learning curve required.
- ❖ Need and cost of acquiring web hosting account.
- ❖ Ability to reach wide spread audience.

4.1 Offline Blog Post Editors

Offline blog post editors provide flexibility to affiliates to save draft copies in local computer.

You can retain a copy of your post in human readable format and preserve HTML formatting. In case your database gets deleted or hacked, then you will be able to restore your blog posts from your local machine. It does not mean that database cannot be read by human beings. It is possible but process of viewing information inside database is more technical. Database management software such as PhpMyAdmin, Ms. Access etc. can be used to extract information from database.

It also provides WYSIWYG editors with commands which may not be available in online blog editors. Wordpress.org has plugins such Ultimate TinyMCE to extend functionality of WordPress blog editor. Wordpress.com does not allow installing plugins. Remember that wordpress.com is different from wordpress.org.

It provides plugins to increase the functionality of your blog post editor. It will enable you to create more professional looking blog posts.

It allows you to publish blog post from your mobile device.

It allows you to reduce dependence on internet connection having all the time. If you are using laptop or mobile at a place where internet connection is not available, you can create blog posts and publish at a later time.

It allows managing multiple blogs created on different blogging platforms from single software. You do not need to visit each blogging platform.

4.2 Security & Backups

Affiliate marketers should keep the record of username and passwords at a place where only you can access them.

If you are running blogs or any other script requiring database. Backup of database should be taken at regular intervals depending on how frequently you post the contents.

Care should be taken when selecting the tools taking database backup that you should be able to restore data successfully without any technical issues.

You should keep the backup of utility used to create backups. Also, you need to keep the backup of all softwares and plugins. So that if vendors discontinue the version of your software and the software at all, you will be able to use it.

4.3 Not Making Use Of Free Plugins And Productivity Tools.

Affiliate marketer should actively look for new plugins to increase productivity. Today, plugins are available for virtually every marketing activity. If affiliate has doubt about the availability of plugins for particular activity, then you must search for it in the community website such as joomla.org, wordpress.org etc.

Plugins should be used with caution. Plugins can make your website instable, increase the page loading time and insecure as well. Backups should be made before installing the plugin.

Review should be carried out about the compatibility of the plugin, effectiveness regarding doing particular tasks etc.

4.4 Non-Compliance With Rules

Violating terms of service of marketplaces, forums, social networking websites etc.

Violating terms of service of marketplaces can ban your account. In that case, all your promotional efforts for affiliate products will go waste. Even, if you open another account, the contents you have posted on forums and social networking site will become lost.

5 VPN and Proxy Servers

VPN (Virtual Private Network) is used to securely transfer information over the internet. One of the benefits of using VPN is replacing the IP address of your country with another country.

Proxy servers are used for hiding the identity of user by replacing the IP address of user with another IP address.

Both VPN and Proxy servers can be used for accessing websites which is banned in your country, such as YouTube, Facebook are banned in some countries.

Both VPN and proxy servers can have different level of anonymity. Paid services provide both higher level anonymity and performance.

VPN is considered better technology for browsing content such as videos that require high speed internet.

Social networking websites, forums and other websites use IP address to limit number of accounts and ban user access to their websites. There are also other methods to ban user as well such as username & email.

VPN can be used to access free resources over the internet such as torrent websites to download training materials, plugins and softwares. Please use VPN and torrents at your own risk.

Numerous VPN applications are available for Windows, Android, Mac etc. platforms.

6   Meta Tags

Meta tags are used provide useful information to web-browsers, search engines and social networking websites. Meta tags can be used to:

- ❖ Communicate language of webpage such as UK or US English.
- ❖ Redirect visitors to different webpage (not recommended, instead use .htaccess file).

- ❖ Restrict crawler (search engine) access to individual webpage. It is up to search engines to honor the request. Spam bots may not be blocked using meta tags (.htaccess file can be used instead to block spam bots).
- ❖ Tell search engine about the original source of duplicate content.
- ❖ Preserve link juice from passing to external website.
- ❖ Tell search engine about the keywords of your webpage. It is no longer used by major search engines, but it is still useful (see below).
- ❖ Provide description of contents of the webpage.

Meta tags are not visible on the face of the webpage. They can be visible to visitors in some cases such as Meta description used as webpage description in search engine results and social networking sites such as Facebook, LinkedIn etc. below the post. Most search engines such as Google and Bing are capable of generating web page description on its own from contents of the web page.

6.1 Nofollow/Dofollow

Nofollow Meta tag enables you to link to external website without providing the link juice and bearing the risk of linking to bad neighborhood. Links from nofollow websites can be counted as backlink but they will not contribute towards improvement to your page rank for search engine optimization.

Affiliate can add no follow tags to affiliate links to avoid providing the backlink. Linking to website involved in black hat (wrongful) SEO practice can lead to penalties from search engines. Nofollow tag provides the solution to this problem.

HTML code for nofollow meta tag is as follows:

```
<meta name='robots' content='nofollow'/>
```

Above tag will be placed between <head> </head> section of HTML web page.

```
<a href="http://example.com" title="Go To Home" rel="nofollow">Home</a>
```

```
<img src=="http://example.com/image/home-button.gif" title="home button" rel="nofollow">
```

To make particular hyperlink nofollow rather than all hyperlink from particular webpage, it will be placed inside HTML tag used to create hyperlink.

Websites are dofollow by default. If an affiliate is interested in building backlinks to increase search engine ranking, then affiliate should make sure that external website linking to his/her website is not nofollow.

6.2 Meta Noindex

It creates the same effect as robots.txt file.

Meta noindex tag restricts the crawler access to web page. Do not use this meta tag on pages you want to get indexed by search engines.

Meta noindex tags are useful for blocking crawler access to webpages requiring password to access. It is better to tell search engines noindex to prevent search engine consider webpage inaccessible by user due to error on webpage.

```
<meta name='robots' content='noindex'/>
```

Above tag will be placed between <head> </head> section of HTML web page.

6.3 Meta Description

Meta description provides information to search engines about the contents of webpage. Meta description needs to be set individually for each webpage.

Webpage Meta description should contain the keywords for which you want appear your website in search engines results. Remember that meta description is also visible to public as search engines may use meta description as an excerpt in the results.

Meta description is also used by popular social networking websites. When visitors share your website link, social networking website automatically adds meta description below the post.

Meta description is used by social bookmarking websites and can be visible to other users to provide brief description of the bookmark and enable user to search relevant bookmarks using search box.

Meta description can be as long as you want. However, most search engines only consider maximum of 155 characters including spaces for generating excerpts. All your important keywords and phrases should be included in first 155 characters including spaces. Each search engine and social networking website has its own limits to the maximum length of meta description.

HTML code for meta description is as follows

`<meta name='description' content='Description Text' />`

6.4 Meta Keyword

Meta keyword tag is no longer used by major search engines. You may use meta keywords for your own records.

`<meta name='keywords' content='Keywords, with or without comma' />`

Social bookmarking websites still relies on keyword meta tag. They provide you with field referred as Tags to write keywords relevant to content (web page, video, ebook etc.).

Therefore, providing Tags in these social bookmarking websites help other users to visit your bookmarked website.

7 Managing Performance as Affiliate

There are many plugins and standalone softwares allow capturing statistical information. Each software provides varying degree of accuracy and timeliness depending on the method they use for capturing information.

Google analytics is very useful to track performance of your various search engine optimization, social media optimization, mass mailing campaigns. Affiliate can get information regarding effectiveness of marketing campaigns in terms of driving traffic, bounce rate (visitors returned from first page visited) etc. It will help you to direct internet marketing efforts, time and money to campaigns providing most favorable results.

Affiliate can create campaigns based on different keywords to see which keywords are most effective for attracting customers. Affiliate can use information of most effective keywords for promoting existing and other similar products.

Affiliate can also create campaigns based on links to different webpages of your website to see which contents leads to highest click on affiliate links and highest click through rate. It will enable you to create more contents that lead to highest click on affiliate links and click through rate.

Affiliate can use analytical information provided from affiliate marketing programs. Analytical information could be:

Number of referrals from your affiliate links. It enables affiliate to determine the effectiveness of internet marketing campaign. If an affiliate is using different marketing strategies for similar products, then affiliate can choose the marketing strategy worked for affiliate products resulting in highest referrals from your affiliate link.

Number of sales made through your affiliate links. Affiliate can compare sales volume of affiliate products to determine which affiliate products achieve highest sales volume through his/her referral or conversion rate. Affiliate can direct his/her resources and skills towards best performing products.

% percentage of referrals converted into sale. Lower conversion rate either implies that you are referring to wrong visitors or vendor is not able to effectively convert visitor into sales.

If affiliate have lower conversion rate on most affiliate products than it means that affiliate is referring wrong visitors.

Amount of commission earned during the period. Affiliate product may have lower referral rate and conversion rate but may be instead generating sufficient earnings. It means, affiliate product generating $100 per month for 1 unit sold is better to promote affiliate product generating $90 per month of 10 units sold.

However, high value/low sales volume products are subject to higher risk. If sales volume is reduced by 1 unit, then sales for the month will be $0. Whereas in case of low value/high sales volume products, if sales volume is decreased by 1 unit, then sales for the month will decrease to $81 only.

Part B: VENDORS

AFFILIATE MARKETING FOR VENDORS

1   Affiliate Marketing for Vendors

Vendors having lack of knowledge on internet marketing can outsource marketing of their products to affiliate marketers.

Affiliate marketing does not lead to cash outflow regardless of making sales as in case of pay per click advertising and fixed payment advertising. Affiliate marketing only involves cash outflow when sale is successfully completed. Therefore, it transfers some of the risk of product failure to affiliates. Vendors will only loose the time and money spent on developing product and recruiting affiliates.

Affiliate marketing program requires only one-off cost to attract suitable affiliates that may provide ongoing sales revenue till foreseeable future.

Many authors and professionals use affiliate marketing to bypass online bookstores to increase share of profit in value network (explained earlier).

2 In-house or Outsourcing Affiliate Program

Vendors can outsource marketing function to outside affiliate program or establish its own affiliate program in-house.

Establishing in-house program depends on:

- Cost and time required to implement and manage the program,
- The need to create single tier or multi-tier program,
- Need to obtain contact information of affiliate for long term relationship,
- Avoiding terms and conditions imposed by outsourcing affiliate program provider.

In-house affiliate program requires initial establishment time to design processes, internal controls and recruiting affiliate program manager. However, in the long term, it may payback initial investments by savings in commission charged by external affiliate program provider.

Through in-house affiliate program, vendor can maintain relationships with your affiliates more effectively. Outsourcing affiliate programs tend to limit communication between vendors and affiliates to continue providing services as an affiliate program provider and controls what information is communicated to affiliates.

Choice of in-house or external affiliate program depends on the sales volume, skills and resources available to vendor.

Third party affiliate program usually provides analytics to measure performance of affiliate program.

Many super affiliates prefer to participate in third party affiliate programs due to third party safeguarding their commission from theft, savings in administration time taken to comply with terms of service and follow up affiliate programs offered by individual vendors to ensure timely payments.

To get super affiliates to promote your products by signing up using in-house affiliate program requires excellent long established reputation and persuasion skills. In addition, product must be of quality, type and value to attract super affiliates.

3 How To Select Affiliate Program For Vendors

Following factors should be considered while selecting affiliate program

3.1 Commission Spread

Highest commission and lowest commission payable to affiliates.

3.2 Competition B/W Vendor in Market Niche

If competition between vendors in market niche relevant to vendor is high, then higher time and money needs to be spent attracting affiliates.

However, lower competition could be an indication lack of affiliates available to promote products in that market niche.

3.3 Ranking Of Vendors

Formula or Filters which affiliate program offers to rank and find vendor also affects the ability to attract affiliates through marketplace or directory at affiliate program provider.

Vendors should consider how his/her product is able to obtain higher ranking or found by affiliates in particular affiliate program.

Affiliate program offering search options or filters or navigation menu to find recently signed up vendors would help vendor to introduce him/herself to existing affiliates.

Vendor needs to understand the algorithm that marketplace is using to rank the products. Similar to SEO for search engines, you need to perform SEO for marketplace in which your product is listed.

Vendor may consider making payment for getting their product listed higher on marketplace providing marketplace has this feature.

3.4   Methods Of Getting Payment

Affiliate program should have low cost, speedy and secured methods for payment. Commonly used payment methods are

- ❖ PayPal
- ❖ Payoneer
- ❖ Check

❖ Wire transfer

Services like PayPal and Payoneer are considered more suitable options because it transfers the money instantly, cheaply and securely

Checks are cheaper than wire transfer but costly than PayPal and Payoneer. Check also requires more time to receive money and can be stolen or bounced.

Wire transfer is the most expensive method for receiving money. However, it transfers money instantly and securely.

Please check before signing up to the marketplace that marketplace provides your required mode of payment and their charges for sending money.

3.5   Transaction Cost Of Getting Payment

Transaction cost of getting payment is necessary to consider as it will reduce the net payment obtained.

Transaction cost or commission per sale charged for running affiliate program.

Transaction cost of credit card processing should be consistent which your product pricing strategy.

If vendor has high value/low sales volume products, then transaction cost on % of sales basis would be more appropriate.

If vendor has low value/high sales volume products, then transaction cost based on fixed monthly charges would be more appropriate.

Vendor having demand pattern affected by seasonal and economic downturn would consider transaction cost on % of sales basis.

Vendor having demand pattern stable through the year and less affected by economic downturn would consider transaction cost based on fixed monthly charges.

In addition, transaction cost charged by different credit card processors needs to be compared.

3.6　Payout Threshold

Payout threshold is minimum account balance which is necessary to become entitled to receive payments. High payment threshold will result in loss of interest or delayed re-investment.

Payout Threshold also limits the losses of theft if your account is hacked or banned or check is stolen in transit.

3.7 Payment Options For Buyers

Payment options available for buyers should be consistent with the geo-locations targeted by vendor.

Payments options can be debit/credit cards, wire transfer, check, cash on delivery, integration with other payment processing companies such as PayPal.

If your targeted geo-location is developing country where fewer people have credit cards and most of the purchases are made by cash on delivery, then your payment processor must support this payment option.

3.8 Taxes

Taxes are one of the most important things you need consider when signing up for payment processing or marketplace. The policy of charging VAT to customer in certain jurisdiction such as EU and policies for deducting withholding taxes before sending money to your account.

Tax is the material item of expenditure you need to consider which can greatly impact your net profit.

3.9 Initial Cost Of Signup

Initial cost of signup should be considered and right to get refund in case your application is disapproved by the affiliate program.

In this respect Click2sell does not have any charges for signing up. It offers great support to new vendors trying to establish their online business.

3.10 Number Of Webpages Or Websites Supported Per Account

If vendor has more than one product page, then vendor should seek affiliate program supporting all webpages for affiliate marketing purpose.

If vendor has more than one website, then vendor should seek affiliate program that allow add more than one website per account for affiliate marketing purpose else vendors needs to setup different account for each website In case if vendor has more than one website, it is much better to find a service that supports multiple website rather than opening account for each individual website. Opening account for each individual website will lead to increased management time, delayed payments until the threshold is reached and more bank charges for receiving payments.

3.11 Integrating Accounts

Sometimes vendor is also an affiliate marketer in the same marketplace or vendor may want to introduce their affiliates to his/her other accounts with the same affiliate program. In such cases, ability to integrate more than one account is of great importance.

3.12 Communication With Affiliates

Vendor may want to communicate new product launch or new resources offered at vendor website. Vendor should determine that either he/she want direct access to contact details of his/her affiliates or he/she will be satisfied to communicate with affiliates through affiliate program.

3.13 Statistical Information

Statistical information can help vendor to target particular market segments such as by country, by product price, by product type etc.

Statistical information will also help vendors the effectiveness of affiliate program for selling his/her products and to make sure that time and money spent on attracting affiliates does not exceed benefit from affiliates.

3.14 Ease Of Purchase Processing

Purchase processing involving lengthy steps such as registration, large number of fields to fill or steps to checkout, personal information, purchase confirmation etc. deters buyer from purchasing.

Fewer and easier the payment process lesser will be the instance of cart abandonment.

3.15 Terms Of Service

Terms of service regarding pricing, discounts, refunds, privacy, commission, subsequent changes to commission offered, upselling and down selling, testimonials, banned products, type of product (digital, shippable, recurring subscription), number of products should be carefully read by vendor to make it is consistent with his/her marketing strategy.

3.16 Countries Supported

Vendor should make sure that affiliate program supports all countries targeted by vendor.

3.17 Access to Customer Information

Vendor may require customer information to sell his/her own existing and new products or affiliate products.

4 How To Attract High Quality Affiliates

4.1 Provide Affiliates With Generous Commission

Different marketplaces offering affiliate programs have different standards for commission.

Example

ClickBank allows commission of minimum 25% and maximum 75% per sale. Amazon provides commission of 4% - 8% per sale depending on the volume of sales.

Commission offered to affiliates must be sufficient according to marketplace standard. Higher commission will enable vendor to attract more affiliates that will result in increased sale volume.

Lower commission will enable vendor to retain high sales margin that will result in increased sales revenue. Ideally, commission should be set at a level that will increase overall earnings.

Higher commission to affiliate increases the requirement for number of sales to be made through affiliate referral to earn profit after deducting the cost incurred in recruiting the affiliate.

Competitors can provide useful clue about the level of commission that would be payable to affiliates. Level of competition between vendors in a market niche etc. can be used to determine the level of commission.

4.2   Provide Affiliates With Multi-Tier Affiliate Program

Affiliates prefer multi-tier programs, as they have share in earnings of affiliates who register to affiliate program through their referral.

Multi-tier program will lead to extra cost of commission payable to 1st tier affiliate on each sale made through referral of 2nd tier affiliates. However, it can result in much larger network of affiliates as higher tier affiliates are also attracting other affiliates to generate earnings from referral made by lower tier affiliates.

Idea behind multi-tier affiliate marketing program is to create viral marketing. It will quickly create the army of affiliates in small amount of time.

4.3 Provide Affiliate Tools & Resources

Provide affiliates tools and resources such as keywords, banners, articles, backlinks, marketing plan etc.

Affiliate invests their time and money to promote affiliate products. Therefore, they may be reluctant to promote new products. However, if vendor can minimize startup time by provide affiliate resources, then affiliates are much likely to promote vendor products.

Creating resources such as banners, ebooks, keywords, useful websites and software requires only one time cost. However, it will increase your sales revenue till foreseeable future.

If affiliates would have to create these resources on their own, then affiliates are likely to demand higher amount of commission. They may agree on lower commission, if these resources were provided.

5 Maintaining Relationship with Affiliates

Maintaining relationship is vital for success of affiliate program and long term earnings. If you use third party affiliate program, you need to obtain contact information of affiliates to follow up for new products and affiliate resources even if you change your affiliate program provider. Contact details will enable you to transfer affiliates to new affiliates program.

If your marketplace does not provide access to affiliate contact details, then you can offer an affiliate a free gift or access to promotional materials related to your product in exchange of contact information such as email, phone etc.

6 Setting Amount of Commission

Level of commission depends on following factors.

6.1 Number of Products

Vendor having more products can reduce the commission payable as affiliates have higher chances of being paid. Even, if visitor do not purchase the product referred by affiliate, he/she may purchase other product from vendor.

6.2 Level of Competition

Higher the level of competition in market niche more commission you have to offer to attract super affiliates.

6.3 Type of Products

Subscription based products can offer lower % of commission then standard product. Affiliate may prefer to earn small amount of commission till foreseeable future which can result in total earnings from subscription based product being higher than commission earnings from standard product.

Example:

Web hosting, membership sites etc.

6.4   Resources

Vendor providing resources such as banners, articles, keywords, free ebooks, testimonials etc. can reduce the level of commission. Affiliates may be still willing to promote affiliate product to account for savings in initial setup time and cost of creating resources.

Creating these resources can lead to one off cost to vendor. However, it can result in savings in commission paid to affiliates and minimize the time taken to make sales through new affiliate.

6.5   Reputation from Existing Business

Vendor having reputation of offline business or other online business can reduce the level of commission. Affiliate may still be willing to promote the product due to low risk associated with promoting the product.

Customers are already aware of the vendor through prior dealings but may not aware of new products launched by the vendor.

COPYRIGHT NOTICE

Copyright © 2019 Murtaza Lanewala. All rights reserved.

www.ingramcontent.com/pod-product-compliance
Lightning Source LLC
Chambersburg PA
CBHW030646220526
45463CB00005B/1658